Get to know
MONEY

A fun, visual guide to how money works and how to manage it

Written by Kalpana Fitzpatrick
Illustrated by Gus Scott

Contents

DK | Penguin Random House

Author Kalpana Fitzpatrick
Illustrator Gus Scott
Editor John Hort
US Editor Jill Hamilton
US Senior Editor Shannon Beatty
Designers Clare Baggaley, Charlotte Jennings, Holly Price
Design Assistance Nidhi Mehra
Managing Editor Jonathan Melmoth
Managing Art Editor Diane Peyton Jones
Production Editor Dragana Puvacic
Production Controller John Casey
Jacket Designer Charlotte Jennings
Economics consultant Niall Kishtainy
Deputy Art Director Mabel Chan
Publishing Director Sarah Larter

First American Edition, 2022
Published in the United States by DK Publishing
1745 Broadway, 20th Floor, New York, NY 10019

Copyright © 2022 Dorling Kindersley Limited
DK, a Division of Penguin Random House LLC
22 23 24 25 26 10 9 8 7 6 5 4 3 2 1
001–321272–Dec/2022

Artwork copyright © Gus Scott, 2022

A catalog record for this book
is available from the Library of Congress.
ISBN 978-0-7440-3497-4

DK books are available at special discounts when
purchased in bulk for sales promotions, premiums,
fund-raising, or educational use. For details, contact:
DK Publishing Special Markets,
1745 Broadway, 20th Floor, New York, NY 10019
SpecialSales@dk.com

Printed and bound in China

For the curious
www.dk.com

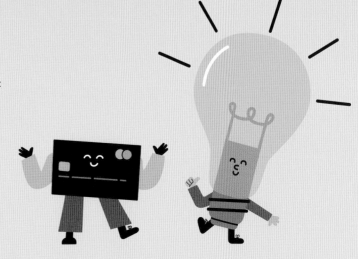

MIX
Paper | Supporting
responsible forestry
FSC™ C018179

This book was made with Forest
Stewardship Council™ certified
paper – one small step in DK's
commitment to a sustainable future.
For more information go to
www.dk.com/our-green-pledge

What is money?

Money is everywhere, but have you ever stopped to think about what it actually is?

The simple answer is that money is something that you can exchange for things. But there is much more to money than meets the eye...

Introducing money

Money is used in almost all countries around the world. It has a set value, which means it is worth the same to everyone who uses it.

Why money works

Money functions because of three main qualities.

Exchangeable

Money is used as a medium of exchange. This means that we can swap money for items that we want. This is what happens when we buy things.

Storable

As money has a set value, it can be stored, and it will be worth the same amount whenever it is used.

Measurable

Money is used to measure the value of things. An item that costs more money is more valuable than an item that costs less.

Money on the move

Money is widely accepted around the world as a form of payment, so it can be moved easily from...

... person to person...

... business to business...

... and government to government.

Built on trust

Money works on trust—when you receive it, you trust that you will be able to exchange it for something you want later on.

Money is supplied and managed by a country's government and central (main) bank. This helps make it trustworthy.

You can learn more about central banks on page 69.

Money through time

Today, we think of money as mainly coins and dollar bills, but it hasn't always been this way. Money has developed and changed throughout human history.

9000 BCE

As society progressed, types of **currency** developed. A currency is something that people agree can be exchanged for goods. Early currencies included feathers and shells.

Before money developed, it is believed that people used **bartering**. This is when you swap one item for another. The use of bartering was first recorded in Egypt.

1200 BCE

China was one of the first countries to use metal as money. These were the first **coins**.

1100 BCE

The first official coinage was called the **Lydian Stater**. These coins were made in Lydia (now Turkey).

600 BCE

1661

Stockholms Banco, a bank in Sweden, become the first European bank to print paper notes.

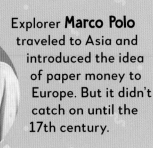

Explorer **Marco Polo** traveled to Asia and introduced the idea of paper money to Europe. But it didn't catch on until the 17th century.

1200

The **gold standard** system made sure that paper money could be exchanged for real gold stored by the government if necessary. It helped people trust the value of paper money.

1871

700 CE

1971

In the 20th century, too much money was printed for it to be linked to gold, and the gold standard ended. We still have paper money, known as **fiat money**, with governments deciding its value.

Paper money was first used in China during the Tang and Song dynasties. It was made from the bark of a mulberry tree.

All about cash

Cash is money in coins or notes. Each type of coin and note has a different value, with notes usually being worth more than coins.

Cash in hand

Cash comes in many different weights, materials, and sizes. It is carefully designed to be durable and easy to use.

Paper notes

Notes are not actually made from paper, but usually from cotton paper or plastic. Cotton notes are easy to fold, carry, and store, as well as being cheap to produce. Plastic is a thin, flexible material that is also waterproof.

Pretty pictures

Notes and coins can have all kinds of images on them that relate to a country's identity. They can show politicians, artists, scientists, wildlife, or even commemorate special events.

25-cent coin from the US

South African 1 rand coin

Tough coins

Coins are mainly made of metals, such as nickel, copper, and zinc. This is because they have to be strong and long-lasting.

Hologram

Foiling

Complicated patterns

Special inks

Printed on specific paper or plastic

Fighting forgery

Cash has security features to stop people from copying it or making their own, which is called forgery. Forged money is illegal.

World's smallest coin

Issued in 2020, this coin was inspired by Albert Einstein's determination during his work as a scientist.

Name: ¼ franc
Where: Switzerland
Size: 0.12 in (2.96mm)
Weight: 0.002 oz (0.063 g)

Actual size!

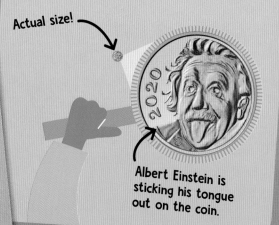

Albert Einstein is sticking his tongue out on the coin.

World's largest coin

Made in 2011, this Australian gold coin is worth A$1,000,000.

Name: The Australian kangaroo
Where: Australia
Width: 31.5 in (80cm)
Weight: 2,231 lb (1,012 kg)

You can learn more about printing money on pages 68-69.

11

Digital money

Digital money can't be held or touched —it exists only in electronic form. It can be spent, saved, and tracked using computers and the internet.

Digital money is worth just as much as cash, so look after it!

Why digital?

Physical cash can be heavy or difficult to carry in large amounts, might easily be damaged or lost, and can't be used online. Digital money has none of these problems—it is just a number on a computer screen.

Following the money

Digital money is kept in a bank account, which is often linked to a physical bank card.

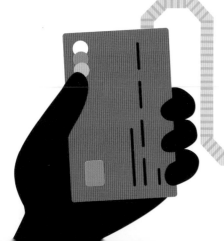

When you buy something using your debit card, the amount it costs is taken out of your bank account and put into the seller's account.

Using digital money

There are a number of ways you can use digital money.

Learn more about bank accounts on pages 30–31.

Mobile phone

Some phones can be used to pay for things, just like a bank card. Fingerprint scanning or facial recognition make sure it's the account owner who is paying.

Digital to physical

You can use your bank card in an ATM (automated teller machine) to change digital money into paper money, or the other way around.

Contactless bank card

You can tap these cards onto a machine to make payments.

 You can tell a card is contactless when it has this symbol on it:

Cashless society

Digital money is so convenient, that some people believe it will replace cash altogether.

World money

The system of money used in a particular country is known as its currency. Many countries have their own currency, while some countries share a currency.

Going abroad

If you visit another country, you need the currency of that country to buy things while you are there.

There are 180 currencies in the world.

Changing money

MONEY EXCHANGE

$1
1 DOLLAR

BUYS

78 RUPEES
7 YUAN
1 EURO

THIS MEANS YOU GET 7 YUAN FOR EVERY 1 DOLLAR YOU EXCHANGE.

Every currency has a different value. To compare the values, we use **exchange rates**.

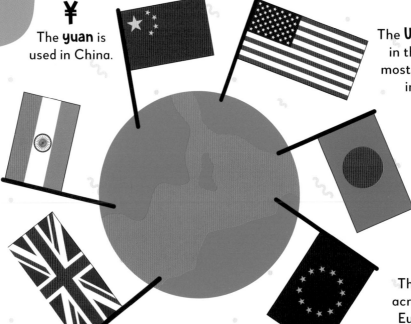

¥
The **yuan** is used in China.

₹
The **rupee** is used in India.

£
The **pound** is used in the UK.

$
The **US dollar** is used in the US. It is the most-used currency in the world.

৳
The **taka** is used in Bangladesh.

€
The **euro** is used across most of the European Union.

Up and down

Some currencies have a higher value than other currencies. However, exchange rates change regularly, which means that the value of a currency can also change over time.

A **strong** currency has a high value. You need less of your own currency to buy a set amount of another currency.

£1 = $3

£1 = $2

When a currency's value doesn't change much, it is **stable**.

£1 = $1

If the value drops, the currency gets **weaker**. To buy a set amount of another currency, you will need more of your own.

A STRONG CURRENCY IS NOT NECESSARILY GOOD NEWS FOR A COUNTRY. IT CAN PUT OFF FOREIGN PEOPLE FROM VISITING AND BUYING THINGS, BECAUSE THEY ARE MORE EXPENSIVE.

You can learn more about economies on pages 60–63.

Why do exchange rates change?

When many people buy a currency, there is a lot of demand for it and its value goes up. If people don't want to buy a currency, its value goes down.

Events

If bad things happen, such as a natural disaster or war, a currency loses value.

Governments

Governments make decisions that change how much a currency is worth.

The economy

If a country has a healthy economy, the currency usually gets stronger.

Quirky currency

Money can be much more than notes and coins. Here are some of the things used as money in different parts of the world and across human history.

Tea bricks

People in Asia made bricks out of tea, which they exchanged for goods. The tea bricks could also be eaten, or used as medicine to treat colds and coughs.

Rai stones are still used for traditional payments or gifts between the Yapese people.

Rai stones

These huge, round stones were used to pay for important things, such as a marriage or funeral. They were dug up in Palau, an island country in the western Pacific Ocean, and taken to the Yap islands in Micronesia.

Whale tooth

In Fiji, polished whale teeth were a symbol of wealth. They could be exchanged for big things, like a canoe. They also made great gifts.

Jade stones

In Asia, jade stones were used as money because they were rare and beautiful. Many of the best pieces of jade stones came from Khotan, in northwest China.

Bafia potato mashers

The Bafia people of West Africa used to make their potato mashers out of iron. In the late 1800s, the potato mashers were highly prized, and were used as a currency for rare and symbolic transactions.

Quetzal bird feathers

The stunning, long, green-and-blue feathers from the quetzal bird of Central America were used to pay for things in Mayan culture. To this day, the money in Guatemala is called quetzal to honor the bird.

Tulips

In the early 1600s, tulips were introduced to the Netherlands from Asia. As they were tricky to grow and extremely popular, they became expensive to trade.

Cowrie shells

Like jade stones, cowrie shells were also pretty and rare, and were used as money in Asia and Africa. People liked them because they were decorative and could be used to make jewelry.

At the peak of their value, one tulip bulb was worth more than a house!

17

Managing money

The way you spend, save, and protect your money is known as personal finance.

Being able to manage your personal finances is a very important skill. If you look after your money well, you will have more of it to use for the things you want and need.

Money choices

Managing money can be tricky. But making the right financial decisions goes a long way if you want to have a healthy and secure future.

Spend or save

If you have money, you can choose to spend it or save it.

Spending

Spending money is an important part of life. Once it is spent the money is gone, so it can be useful to plan your spending.

Savings

The money we keep is called savings. Money can be saved in a money box, in the bank, or even in an investment. You will learn more about savings throughout this chapter.

Heat

Needs

These are things you need to stay alive, such as food, water, and a home.

Shelter

Clean water

Nutritious food

Clothes

Needs
or wants?

When making money decisions, it can be helpful to think of things as wants and needs. It can stop you from spending too much, and help you focus on the important things.

Vacations

Gadgets

Wants

These are things you would like to have, such as games or chocolates. They are nice to have. but you don't need them to live.

Sports cars

Games

Spending

The most common thing people do with money is spend it. That means swapping money for goods or services.

Goods

Things that can be held or touched are called goods. These include all the things you see on store shelves.

Value for money

The cheapest option isn't always the best choice! Consider the quality of what you are buying, and how it has been made.

Books

Toys

Sports goods

Cereal

Cans

Drinks

Fresh produce

Bread

VERY SIMILAR ITEMS MIGHT BE QUITE DIFFERENT IN PRICE! COMPARE PRICES TO MAKE SURE YOU ARE MAKING THE RIGHT CHOICE.

These **organic** products are made in a way that is kinder to animals and our planet.

The workers who made this were paid **fairly**.

Transporting this from a **local** producer didn't use much energy, which is good for the environment.

Services

The other main way you can spend money is to pay someone to do something for you. This is called a service.

HAIR CUT $10

Some services you need...

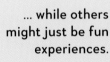
BALLOON RIDE $140

... while others might just be fun experiences.

Services usually cost more if they require expensive equipment or training.

Undercover costs

Even when you buy goods, you are usually paying for services, too. The price of an apple might include:

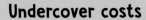

60¢

 GROWING – 10¢

 PICKING – 5¢

 PACKAGING – 5¢

 TRANSPORT – 10¢

 STORE COSTS – 10¢

 STORE STAFF – 10¢

Any money left over is kept by the store as profit.

Governments spend money too. Find out more on pages 64–65.

23

Planting your savings

Savings are like planting a tree—you may not be able to enjoy the tree right away, but the shelter the tree provides may be useful in the future. There are three categories of saving.

For purchases

Sometimes, you may want to save up to buy something, like a new bike, or a trip, like a visit to a water park. Without savings, it would be impossible to pay for these things.

Adults save for big purchases, such as a house or a wedding.

Super savings

When we earn money it is important to keep some of it. This is called saving.

For a rainy day

Sometimes, unfortunate things happen that can cost a lot of money, such as a car breaking down or a roof leaking. If you have savings, you can use the money to pay for emergencies.

For the future

The most common way people save for the future is with a pension. A pension is a special savings plan that helps give you money when you retire. When you work for an employer, they may contribute into your pension savings pot.

It is always a good idea to have a pension as an adult, even if retirement is a long way away.

Your pension money is also invested for you. You can learn more about investing on pages 50–51.

How to save

Saving can be difficult when there are so many important things that need to be paid for. But there are a few things you can do to make saving easier.

Steps to save

Here are four steps you can take to save your money:

Picture your goals

Think about things you'd like to buy and how much money you'll need to pay for them.

Plan your spending

Creating a budget helps you to plan ahead. You can decide what to spend and what to save.

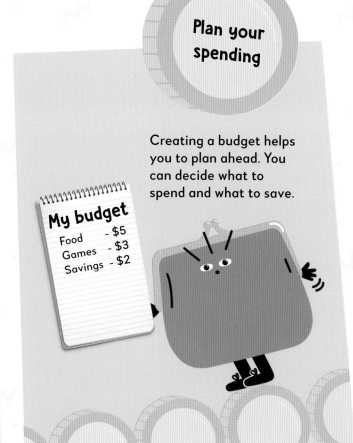

My budget
Food   - $5
Games   - $3
Savings - $2

Putting your spare change or pocket money into a money box is a good way to start saving.

Grow your money

There are many ways to help your money grow. If you store it in a bank, the bank will pay you extra money, called interest.

You can learn more about interest on pages 32–33.

Spend less

Cutting down on your spending is a great way to save money. Think about what you really need, and try not to waste money.

STORES

A simple plan

If you are not sure of the best way to budget, you can follow the **50/30/20 rule**.

50%

30%

20%

Keep **50%** of your money for expenses, such as food and bills.

Spend **30%** on whatever you like.

Put **20%** aside as savings.

Try building your own budget on page 91.

Budgeting

A budget is a plan to manage your money. It can help you decide how much to spend and save. A budget is usually based on income (how much money comes in) and expenses (how much money goes out).

EXPENSES

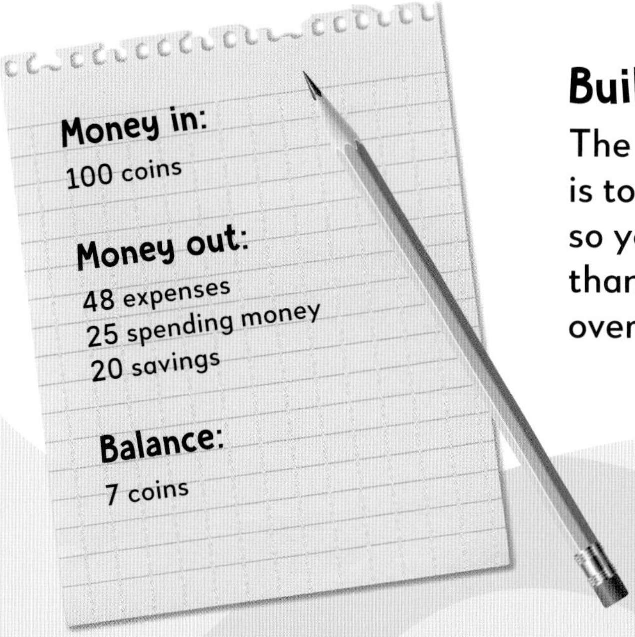

Money in:
100 coins

Money out:
48 expenses
25 spending money
20 savings

Balance:
7 coins

Building a budget

The purpose of a budget is to keep track of money so you don't spend more than you earn. Money left over is called a balance.

It's always good to have a balance left over because it shows you haven't overspent.

SPENDING MONEY

SAVINGS

29

Banking

A bank is a business that looks after people's money. It can also lend money, and helps people pay for things when they use a bank card.

Bank account

Many people store their money in a bank account that can be accessed online, on the phone, or at a building called a branch.

Bank teller

These people work behind the desk at bank branches. Tellers can help you manage your money, for example, if you want to open an account, borrow money, or exchange currency.

Safe

Some banks have a vault, or safe, to hold cash and valuables. Safes are strong and secure, and hidden away within the building. This is to protect the contents from theft and damage.

ATM

An ATM allows you to take cash out of your bank account by inserting your bank card and entering a secure PIN (personal identification number). You should never share your PIN with anyone.

Balance
You can go to your online bank to check how much money you have.

Check out how to stay safe with your money online on pages 36–37.

Account history
Past payments can be seen here.

$20

−$2
Toy store
Pocket money   +$10

Make a payment
You can pay bills or transfer money from your online account.

From: me

$3

To: mom

Customer care
You can still receive help from your bank online, by phoning or messaging them.

Banking online
Online banking lets you keep track of your money through an app or a website. You need to choose a password to access your account online, so that no one else can get into it.

The example below uses an interest rate of 3 percent.

Interesting interest

To encourage you to store your money with them, banks offer to pay you a small amount. This payment is called interest.

Interest rates

The amount, or rate, of interest is usually a fixed percentage of how much money you already have in the account.

TO FIGURE OUT HOW MUCH INTEREST YOU WOULD EARN, DIVIDE THE AMOUNT IN YOUR ACCOUNT BY 100 AND MULTIPLY IT BY THE RATE OF INTEREST.

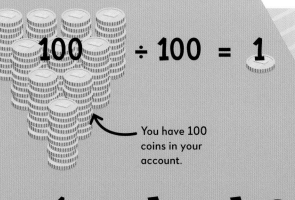

$$100 \div 100 = 1$$

You have 100 coins in your account.

$$1 \times 3 = 3$$

This is your interest payment.

The higher the interest rate, the more money you earn.

$$100 + 3 = 103$$

This is your total, including interest.

Compound interest

Many bank accounts pay compound interest. This is interest that you earn on all your money, including the interest you've already received, so your savings can grow more and more each year.

The more you save, the more you earn!

Year 1
If you have 100 coins and earn 10 percent interest per year, you will have **110 coins** at the end of the first year.

Year 2
In the second year, the 10 percent interest is added to the new amount of 110 coins, so you end up with **121 coins**.

Year 3
The same thing happens in the third year, so 10 percent interest on 121 coins gives you **133 coins**.

Year 10
By the end of 10 years, you would have **259 coins**!

Albert Einstein is believed to have said, "Compound interest is the eighth wonder of the world. He who understands it, earns it; he who doesn't, pays it."

What is debt?

Sometimes, people may need to borrow money to pay for things. The borrowed money is known as debt.

Borrowing

Borrowing is when you receive something for a period of time. You must always return what you borrow.

IMAGINE THAT YOU DON'T HAVE ENOUGH MONEY TO BUY SOMETHING.

YOU COULD BORROW THE MONEY FROM SOMEONE ELSE.

BUT YOU MUST PAY THE FULL AMOUNT BACK, BY A DATE YOU BOTH AGREED ON.

Interest

If you borrow with interest, you will have to give back more than you borrowed.

NOW IMAGINE YOU WANT SOMETHING ELSE, THAT MIGHT COST A LOT OF MONEY.

THE PERSON OR PEOPLE LENDING YOU MONEY MIGHT ASK FOR IT TO BE PAID BACK WITH INTEREST.

IF YOU CANNOT PAY THE MONEY BACK ON TIME, THE INTEREST WILL BUILD UP, AND YOU MAY STRUGGLE TO PAY ALL THE MONEY BACK.

How to borrow

There are a number of ways adults can borrow money.

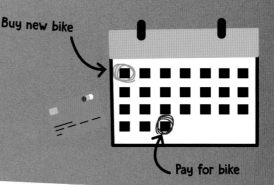

It's not just individuals that borrow money. You can read more about government debt on page 68.

Buying on credit

Credit cards allow people to buy things now, and pay for them later. If payment is not made on time, the credit card company can charge interest and late fees, which can get very expensive.

Buy new bike

Pay for bike

Loans

Some people may take out a loan from a bank, which allows them to borrow money for a period of time. The money has to be paid back, usually with interest.

Mortgages

Property, such as houses and apartments, are very expensive. Usually, the only way to buy one is to get a mortgage. This is when the bank lends you money specifically to buy property, and you must pay back a set amount each month, with interest.

Borrowing money can help pay for important things, such as a home or education. However, debt can build quickly. Only borrow money if you will be able to pay it back.

Money safety

Your money and identity are valuable, and criminals might try to steal it. They may do this by either pretending to be you, or by tricking you into giving them money. This is known as fraud, or a scam.

🔒 COMMON SCAMS

← → C ↑

There are a number of ways fraudsters will try to con you online.

Hacker

This is a person who uses a computer to gain **access** to information without permission.

Vishing

This is when someone **pretends** to be calling from your bank, police, or even the government. They may ask you to transfer money to their account. Hang up.

Phishing

This is when criminals send you a **bogus link** or text. It may look like it's from a genuine sender, but if you click on it, they could steal information and money from you. Delete the message.

Money mule

This is when someone asks you to put **money into your account** for them and then transfer it to another account. Allowing someone to use your account to move money around makes you a money mule, and it is illegal.

WARNING!

DO'S AND DON'TS

DO'S

- DO BE AWARE OF PEOPLE ON SOCIAL MEDIA TELLING YOU ABOUT WAYS YOU CAN MAKE MONEY QUICKLY. THEY ARE USUALLY SCAMS.

- DO HAVE A STRONG PASSWORD, AND DO CHANGE IT EVERY FEW MONTHS, SO HACKERS CAN'T GUESS IT.

- DO CHECK YOUR ACCOUNT REGULARLY TO MAKE SURE NO ONE HAS SPENT YOUR MONEY BY STEALING YOUR DETAILS.

- DO BE AWARE OF FAKE ONLINE STORES CREATED BY FRAUDSTERS. ASK AN ADULT TO CHECK THE URL OF A WEBSITE BEFORE BUYING ANYTHING.

- DO KEEP CASH SAFE, PUT IT AWAY AND OUT OF SIGHT SO NO ONE CAN STEAL IT.

DON'TS

- DON'T CLICK ON UNKNOWN LINKS.

- DON'T ACCESS YOUR BANK ACCOUNT OR MAKE ANY PAYMENTS USING FREE WI-FI. CRIMINALS CAN INTERCEPT WHAT YOU ARE DOING AND STEAL YOUR INFORMATION OR MONEY.

- DON'T BELIEVE ANYONE WHO CALLS YOU UP AND ASKS FOR PERSONAL DETAILS, SUCH AS PASSWORDS.

- DON'T LET OTHER PEOPLE USE YOUR BANK ACCOUNT TO TRANSFER MONEY.

You can learn about other money concerns on pages 78–79.

Making money

Usually, making money involves swapping
something you have—such as a skill,
your time, or an object you own—
in exchange for money.

Many adults do a job or run their own
business, but you can also use the money
you have to make more money by investing it.

Builder

Doctor

Engineer

Chef

Office Worker

The money earned from working is known as wages, or salary.

Different jobs

On average, adults spend around 35 hours a week working, although in some countries this could be as much as 45 hours. So it is good to start thinking about your interests and the things you enjoy, and consider what kind of jobs you might like to do.

Working world

People who are employed get paid for working, or doing a job. The amount of money they earn depends on their education, skills, experience, and the industry, or type of job, they work in.

The career ladder

A career is a job someone does for a long period of time in their life. It usually provides opportunities to move into more senior positions and earn more money. This is known as climbing the career ladder.

Entry-level jobs

School-dropouts can sometimes find entry-level jobs, such as an assistant. As they gain more skills and extra responsibility, they can progress to more senior positions.

Further education

Many professional careers, such as in medicine and teaching, require specialist knowledge and specific qualifications. These can be obtained through further education, such as a university degree or a diploma.

Work experience

Employers may offer placements or volunteer (unpaid) work for people to gain practical experience of a particular job or industry.

Training

Some employers pay for their employees to take training courses alongside their work so they can gain more skills and increase their chances of progressing in their careers.

The legal age for working in most countries is around 16–18 years, although the rules vary in different places.

Introducing entrepreneurs

Some people make money by creating their own jobs. An entrepreneur is someone who starts their own business. Anyone can be an entrepreneur but it can be hard work.

Steve Chen, Chad Hurley, and Jawed Karim

Steve, Chad, and Jawed co-created the social media platform YouTube when they realized there wasn't anywhere for people to share videos online.

Nationalities: American
Company: YouTube
Company value: US$160 billion
Known as: Co-founders

Rihanna

Rihanna is a singer, songwriter, actor, designer, and businesswoman. She launched her cosmetics company Fenty Beauty in 2017.

Nationality: Barbadian
Company: Fenty Beauty
Company value: US$2.8 billion
Known as: CEO

Risk vs reward

Entrepreneurs have to balance risk and reward.

Reward
The goal of entrepreneurs is usually to make profit. This means making more money than they are spending.

Risk
An entrepreneur usually has to spend money to make money, without knowing if they will get it back. This is known as financial risk.

What is a start-up?

A start-up is a new, upcoming business. It can be very difficult to create a start-up.

10%

90%

Around 90 percent of start-ups fail. Businesses fail for many reasons, including a lack of demand for the product or service they are selling, or because they run out of money.

You can learn more about entrepreneurial skills on the next page.

Who can be an entrepreneur?

Anyone! There has even been a 4-year-old whose lemonade recipe made it into hundreds of shops in the US. However, most successful entrepreneurs have some key skills in common. They are:

Adaptable

Creative

Motivated

Well-informed

Passionate

Starting a business

A business is an organization that makes or provides a product or service in exchange for money. Anyone can start one, by following these key steps.

?

Have an idea

Think creatively—what is missing in the world? What do you love or feel strongly about? If you have a passion for your product or service, you will have a better chance of being successful.

Research

Find out if your idea already exists, and work out what your USP (unique selling point) will be—ask yourself what is different or special about your business.

CUPCAKE BUSINESS!

$$$

Some people borrow money to start a business. You can read more about debt on pages 34–35.

It doesn't matter how small or big your idea is—if people like it and it is something they want, then you can be a successful entrepreneur.

Plan

Create a business plan. This will identify how much money you have to spend, and how much you plan on making.

Sell

Offer your product to the public. The price of your product or service will have been decided in your business plan.

Invest

Spend your seed money. This is the money you use to start your business. If you start a cake business, your seed money would buy your ingredients and equipment.

Profit

If more money was made than spent on the business, then the business is in profit.

Loss

If sales do not bring you more money than you have spent, the business will make a loss. Some businesses make a loss before they start to make a profit.

Self-employed

Anyone who owns a business is self-employed, which means they work for themselves rather than doing a job that someone else pays them for.

Money in motion

Every day, hour, minute, and second, money is being spent and earned by individuals and businesses. It flows around in a never-ending cycle.

When households spend money, they are consumers. The money they spend goes to the firms that provide goods or services.

Firms pay the salaries of workers to produce goods or services.

FIRMS

Flowing income

Organizations, called firms, that provide goods and services are known as producers. When someone buys goods or services, they are known as a consumer. The money that people make every day is part of a wider cycle: the flow of goods, services, and money between producers and consumers.

PAYING WAGES

SPENDING

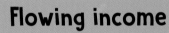

Households put some money into savings, but the rest of the salary is needed to pay for things.

HOUSEHOLDS

The wages paid by firms go to individual people and their households.

Consumer power

Consumers have the power to change the ways producers make money, by spending—or not spending—on certain goods and services.

You can learn more about using money to help society on pages 84–85.

Dollar voting

If one producer acts unethically, consumers can switch to a producer who is more ethical. This is called dollar voting. The first producer then may rethink their business practices because they are losing out on making money.

PROTECT NATURE NOT PROFITS!

A consumer may choose not to spend money with a producer who harms the rainforest.

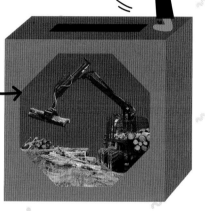

Campaigning

Dollar voting isn't the only way consumers can influence producers. They can protest to raise awareness if a producer is behaving poorly, or they can spread awareness by writing to a local politcian or on social media.

This robotic polar bear was built to protest against companies that harm the environment.

Instead, a producer that is more environmentally friendly will get the consumer's money.

When it comes to making money, producers often keep consumer power in mind.

Supply and demand

Producers adjust their supply, which is the amount of goods or services they make and provide, based on demand. This is the number of people who want to pay the price set by the producer.

What's the price?

Supply and demand influence the price. If demand is higher than supply, producers can increase the price of their goods because there are more people who want to buy them than there are items available.

Supply

A clothing designer wants to sell 10 T-shirts at $20 each.

Demand

If **10 people** want to buy a T-shirt for $20, then demand matches the supply.

$20

$40

Higher

If demand is higher and there are **20 people** who want to buy a T-shirt at $20, the designer could sell them at a higher price to make more money, because there is more demand than supply.

Lower

If demand is lower and only **5 people** want to buy a T-shirt at $20, the designer would have to sell the T-shirts at a lower price because demand is lower than supply.

$10

Demand ups and downs

There are several things that
can cause demand to rise and fall.

Seasons

When it is colder, there is a higher demand for some things, such as thick, wooly clothes.

When the weather warms up, fewer people think about buying winter clothes.

Price changes

A lower price means that more people can afford to buy something.

~~$150~~ $100

$300

A higher price makes an item less affordable, so fewer people will be interested in buying it.

Trends

Some things are in demand because they are trendy, or popular, at the time.

Trends may only last for a short time, which means demand can drop quickly.

Publicity

If something is advertized in the media, it could create a higher demand for something.

If something receives bad publicity, fewer people will want it and demand will drop.

Income

If people's income increases, they may spend more money, which in turn increases demand.

If people's income drops, they will have less money to spend, which means demand will decrease.

Investing

The idea of investing is to buy something that grows in value over time. When you come to sell it, you'll get more money back than you paid. Easy, right?

Risk and reward

If it was that simple, everyone would do it. But all investments involve some risk—you *might* make money, but you *might* lose it.

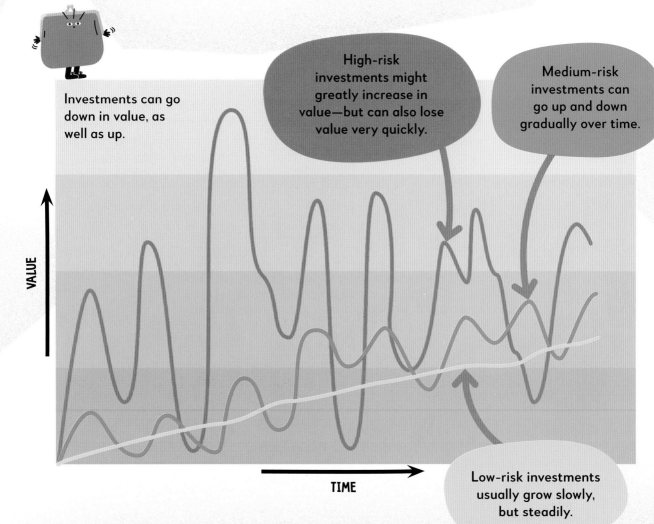

Investments can go down in value, as well as up.

High-risk investments might greatly increase in value—but can also lose value very quickly.

Medium-risk investments can go up and down gradually over time.

VALUE

TIME

Low-risk investments usually grow slowly, but steadily.

How to invest

There are many types of investments that can grow in value.

Buy things

TOY CAR $3.99

What you buy doesn't matter, but try to choose something that might be worth more in future.

REWARD

VINTAGE TOY CAR $50

If it becomes more valuable, you can sell it later for a higher price.

! RISK

But if demand drops, you might make a loss.

SALE $2.50

Rent it out

If you buy something that other people want to use, you can charge them a fee, called rent.

REWARD

TO RENT

When they return it, you still own the item. You can rent it out again, or sell it.

! RISK

What if the renter damages your property? Will it cost a lot to repair or replace it?

Be the bank

BONDS INC.

You can loan money to companies or governments by buying their bonds.

REWARD

A bond is like an IOU. The borrower promises to pay you back later, plus interest.

! RISK

BONDS INC.

But watch out: if the company goes bankrupt, they might not be able to pay you back at all.

Shares

Another popular way to invest is to buy pieces—called shares—of companies. The company might earn you money, and the value of your share might grow, too.

Why buy shares?

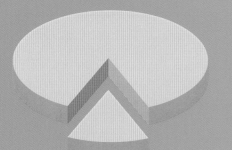

Anyone who buys shares becomes a shareholder, or part-owner of the company.

Successful companies can make lots of money. The people who own the company can take some of this money as rewards, called dividends.

NOT ALL SUCCESSFUL COMPANIES PAY DIVIDENDS. SOME CHOOSE TO SPEND THEIR PROFITS TO TRY TO MAKE EVEN MORE MONEY IN THE FUTURE.

For example, advertizing costs money, but it can help a company sell products to more people.

Rising and falling

If a company is successful, many people want to own a piece of it. They are willing to pay more for shares, so the price goes up.

If the company is not successful, people try to sell their shares, even at a lower price.

10¢ anyone??

The stock market

A company can make its shares available on the stock market, so that anyone can buy or sell them. There is no set price for a share.

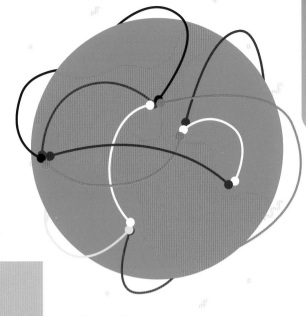

Sell, sell, sell!

To make money, investors try to sell when the share price is high...

Millions of shares are bought and sold every day, all around the world.

A bull market means the economy is doing well. As a result, share prices are going up.

A bear market means the economy is not strong, and share prices are going down.

...and buy when the share price is low.

Buy, buy, buy!

53

Toys and games

From original Monopoly sets to classic Barbies, old toys can be a great investment. A teddy bear from 1904, made by a German company called Steiff, was once sold in Japan for US $171,600.

Collectable cards

Two boxes of sealed Pokémon cards sold at auction for more than $19,000 in the UK.

Unusual investments

Some people invest in things they like, such as comics, artwork, or even handbags. They may buy something that they believe could be worth a lot of money in the future and therefore think is a good investment.

There are no guarantees this kind of investment will ever make money, but if you look after things well, you could sell them in the future.

Comics

A single page from a 1984 Spider-Man comic sold for almost US$3,400,000 in the US at an auction because it had the first black Spidey costume, which led to the Marvel character Venom.

Investments tend to be more valuable if they are rare or one of a kind.

Antiques

Many people invest in antiques. Antiques are collectable objects, such as a piece of art or furniture, that have a high value because of age and quality.

Stamps

A collection of four Chinese stamps from 1897, called the Red Revenue, was sold for US$15.2 million in 2009. The collection and study of stamps is called philately.

Rule 1

Invest early

The sooner you start investing, the more time your money will have to grow because of the effect of compound interest.

Look back at pages 32–33 to learn about compound interest.

Investing rules

Investing is a great way to make your money grow. But there are important rules to follow to do it safely and successfully.

Rule 2

Be patient

Be prepared to hold your money in an investment for a long time. Think of it as like planting a tree—it might take years for it to grow and give you fruit.

Rule 3

Budget carefully

Investments take time to grow, so you should not invest money that you may need for bills, or to buy something in a few months' time.

Rule 5

Diversify

Diversification means investing in many different things. It reduces the chance of losing money, because even if one investment does badly, others may still do well.

Diversification reduces the probability of overall loss because money is spread around.

Rule 4

Understand the investment

Before you invest, you should fully understand what you're investing in and the risks. Do not be pressured into investing in something just because lots of people are talking about it.

Some investments have many terms and conditions. Always make sure you understand and are happy with the small print of an investment, and don't be afraid to ask questions.

Global money

We've already learned about how people and individual businesses use money.

But economics can also be studied on a larger scale, such as how a country produces goods and services and how it spends money.

The economy

The economy is a term used to describe how a country is doing in producing goods and services, and how much money it has. Decisions made by individuals, firms, and governments affect how much an economy produces.

Measuring economies

The economy of a country is usually measured by its Gross Domestic Product (GDP). This is the total value of all the goods and services sold during a certain period, such as a year.

$1.4 trillion

TV and movies

GDP

All the money made from all goods and services you can think of are the GDP of a country.

Businesses

Education

Tourism

Stores

Food produced

Natural resources

Moving prices

Governments keep track of the prices of things to judge how well the economy is doing. Normally, the prices of things steadily increase over time—this is known as inflation.

Inflation

Inflation is normal and it isn't bad. It means the economy of the country is growing. But high inflation can be bad. If prices go too high, it is harder for people to buy things.

Deflation

Deflation is the opposite of inflation. It means prices are going down. This can be bad for the economy, suggesting there is a lack of demand for things that a country is producing.

Interest rates

If inflation gets too high, the country's central bank may increase interest rates. This makes it more expensive to borrow money and encourages people to save instead. As a result, demand may fall, and inflation may go down.

You can learn more about central banks on page 69.

The workforce

Employment is the number of people with jobs. High employment is good—lots of people earning money means lots of people spending money, which keeps the economy healthy.

Governments also keep an eye on wages. If prices go up quicker than wages, people will struggle to afford the things they need.

Human resources

These are workers who are employed by businesses. This is also known as labor. Some examples of human resources are doctors, plumbers, and truck drivers.

Natural resources

These come from nature, and include water, crops, and trees. They are not made by people, although people are needed to extract or harvest them. They are also limited in supply.

Capital resources

These are tools and machines you need to produce goods. Some examples of capital resources are buildings, cranes, and ships.

Building economies

Resources are essential for all economies. They are what we use to make goods and provide services. There are three main types.

Money and resources

Resources have an impact on everyday spending. If the price of resources increases, the price of goods and services can increase, too.

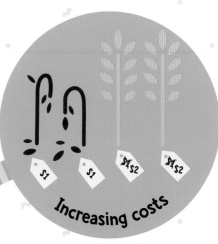

Increasing costs

If there is a bad harvest, the price of wheat might increase because there is a lower supply but the same demand.

The price of bread will need to go up.

Producer problems

The producer will no longer be able to offer the same amount of bread for the same price, because the wheat they used to make the bread is more expensive.

Price increase

Consumers will have to pay more money for the same amount of bread.

63

Government spending

Just like ordinary people and families, governments have to look after money and spend it wisely. There are many things they need to provide for the citizens of their country.

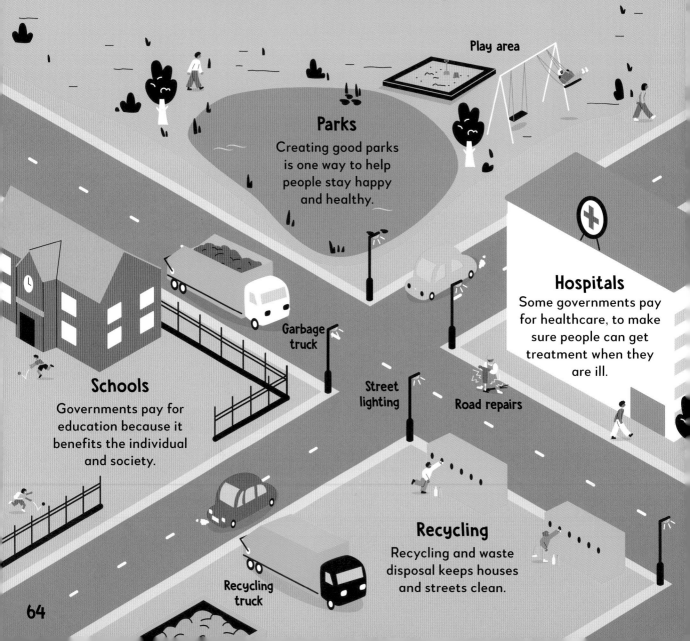

Play area

Parks
Creating good parks is one way to help people stay happy and healthy.

Hospitals
Some governments pay for healthcare, to make sure people can get treatment when they are ill.

Garbage truck

Street lighting

Road repairs

Schools
Governments pay for education because it benefits the individual and society.

Recycling
Recycling and waste disposal keeps houses and streets clean.

Recycling truck

Infrastructure

Infrastructure, such as roads and bridges, are important because they connect people and businesses.

Libraries

Public libraries are paid for by the government, to give everyone access to books.

Water systems

Everybody needs clean water to live. A good water system helps to keep people healthy.

Street cleaner

Fire station

Fire fighter

Fire truck

Police station

Police officer

Emergency services

The government pays for some important services, such as a police force to stop crime, and fire fighters to protect buildings.

Government building

Sidewalks

Big decisions

It's up to the government to decide how to spend money. Citizens expect their government to get good value for money on their spending.

Sewers

Taxing tax

Governments collect money from people by something called tax. The government uses the tax money to pay for services.

Paying tax

Adults pay tax as a contribution to public services that we all use. Paying tax is a legal requirement in most countries. Businesses also pay tax. This is known as **corporate tax**.

Charging tax

There are many different taxes, some large, some small. Often they are charged when money changes hands.

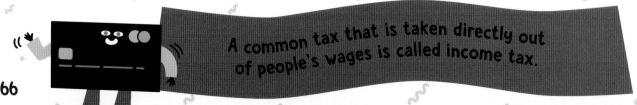

A common tax that is taken directly out of people's wages is called income tax.

Types of tax

As well as income tax, in some countries you pay tax when you buy goods and services. You also pay tax if you make extra money on savings and investments, or buy property.

Fair tax

Not everyone thinks taxes are fair, but governments try to make them as fair as possible. For example, people who earn a higher amount pay more tax.

World's strangest tax

In medieval England, knights could choose not to fight in a war by paying a cowardice tax.

Name: Cowardice tax
Where: England
When: c.1100 CE

World's smelliest tax

In Ancient Rome, urine was used for tanning leather. As a result, the sale of urine was taxed.

Name: Urine tax
Where: Rome, Italy
When: c.70 CE

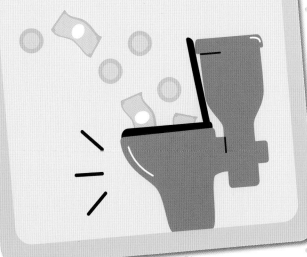

Finding funds

If governments need to raise more money to pay for public services in addition to taxes, they can either borrow or print more money. However, both of these options have downsides.

Borrowing money

Just like individuals, governments can borrow money from banks and other sources. The total amount that a goverment has borrowed is called national debt.

The lenders

Financial institutions demand interest on the money they lend. Given the huge amounts governments borrow, this can make interest payments very expensive.

The borrowers

Governments gain huge amounts of money from taxes, so banks and other financial institutions trust them enough to lend them money.

Almost all governments borrow money— some countries have debts that are in the trillions of US dollars!

Central banks

Most countries have central banks. These banks are often independent of the government, but they do work together. Central banks help make decisions on many things, including printing money.

Often known as the "Fed," the Federal Reserve is the central bank of the US.

Printing money

New banknotes or coins may be made to replace old, worn-out ones. However, some governments also print more money when they need more.

New money

New money is printed every day. Governments try to predict how much money they should print.

Watching inflation

Printing money is not always a good idea—creating more money can cause inflation, and make the currency less valuable.

What is a recession?

If a country's economy is not doing well, it could go into what is known as a recession. This means that the country's GDP is going down, and that its people may become less wealthy.

What causes a recession?

Recessions are caused by many different things, often at the same time. Here are some common causes.

High interest rates

If borrowing costs are too high, people will stop spending money.

Loss of confidence

If consumers don't feel confident spending money, the economy gets weaker.

Unexpected events

An event such as a war or a pandemic can stop an economy from growing.

JOB CENTER

Unemployment

A recession is bad news for people because it can lead to unemployment. If people don't have jobs, they are at risk of poverty. When unemployment is high, people spend less, so the economy produces less.

FINANCIAL NEWS

If companies do really badly and start losing a lot of money, or if many people start withdrawing their money from a bank, it can lead to a financial crisis.

Historical crises

Financial crises are always headline news. They usually affect millions, if not billions of people. Some are so huge that they are considered major historical events.

Unemployed men lining outside a soup kitchen during the Great Depression.

The Great Depression: 1929–1933

The Great Depression started as stock markets crashed and businesses started to lose money. The economy was so weak that many people could not afford food or a home to live in. It started in the US, but spread across the world.

The Great Recession: 2007–2008

The Great Recession started when banks gave mortgages and loans to home buyers who could not afford the repayments. It started in the US, but because other countries invested in American banks, it soon became a global crisis.

An employee of the bankrupt Lehman Brothers investment bank carries a box of belongings out of the company's headquarters in New York City, 2008.

Many businesses closed down as a result of the Great Recession.

Cryptocurrency

Cryptocurrency, or crypto, is a type of digital money. Instead of being controlled by one country's government or central bank, it relies on a special computer code that can be used anywhere. There are many different kinds of cryptocurrency, but the first one was Bitcoin.

Building the blockchain

Crypto transactions involve transferring data, rather than cash. All crypto transactions are publicly recorded, on something called a blockchain.

Cryptocurrencies are made, exchanged, and stored using cryptography, which is the science of codebreaking.

How does a blockchain work?

When a transaction is requested, a new digital block is created, which represents the transaction.

The block is sent to many computers, which approve the transaction.

The block is added to the blockchain, and the whole cryptocurrency network is updated.

The transaction is now on the blockchain, and is now complete!

Where does crypto come from?

To make Bitcoin, somebody has to "mine" it. Mining means using powerful computers to crack a code, which creates a Bitcoin and adds it to the blockchain.

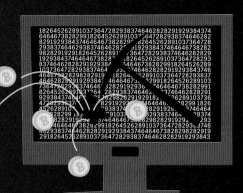

Mining Bitcoin requires powerful computers, which use lots of energy. This is bad for our planet, because much of the energy comes from burning fossil fuels, which causes pollution.

Why crypto?

Cryptocurrency uses modern technologies, which give them unique qualities.

Decentralized

Crypto is maintained by computers, not leaders. This means it is decentralized—a government doesn't control it.

Public

Every transaction is recorded on the public blockchain, so everyone can make sure it is fair.

Security

The special codes crypto uses are very complicated, so it is hard for criminals to cheat the system or steal money.

 Cryptocurrencies have downsides. Their value can rise and fall very quickly, which makes them very unstable currencies, and they cannot be used in most stores.

Mindful money

Money is a big part of life. People who look after money well are much more likely to be confident, successful, and happy.

A good relationship with money is often like a good relationship with a friend: you need to communicate, understand boundaries, and be able to ask for help.

Friendship and money

As you grow up, you might talk to your friends about money. While it is good to talk about money, sometimes mixing finances and friends can cause problems. Here are some tips to help you avoid some common issues.

FOMO!

FOMO stands for "fear of missing out." We often do things not because we want to, but because we think we will miss out on something. But this can become a problem, because you could end up spending more money than you have.

To conquer FOMO, confront it. Be honest with yourself and realistic about what you can afford.

Worry about your own saving goals—don't let other people distract you from them.

If your friends are pressuring you into spending money, then it is OK to say no.

Comparing yourself

It's important to feel gratitude for what you have. Don't worry about what other people have. Everyone has different priorities when it comes to spending money.

Giving money to friends

If a friend wants to borrow money from you, ask a grown-up about it first. If you don't set boundaries and have a clear agreement, lending money can lead to nasty arguments.

> Focus on the positives! Think about all the things you are lucky to have.

> If you don't feel comfortable about lending or borrowing, you should not do it.

> Borrowing and lending money is about trust. If money is not given back on time, it can make a relationship break down.

Money worries

It is natural to worry about money occasionally. Sometimes things happen to us or our families that we can't control. This can make us feel anxious, but understanding common issues can help.

Redundancy

If a company isn't doing well, some workers may lose their jobs. This is known as redundancy. When people are made redundant, they may have to make cutbacks in their spending until they find another job.

Debt

Sometimes, if an adult gets into debt, it can be difficult to keep up with repayments. This might mean they have to cut back on spending until the debt is repaid.

Long-term illness

If people become ill, they may have to take time off work until they feel better. Sometimes, this means they won't be able to earn money while they are not working.

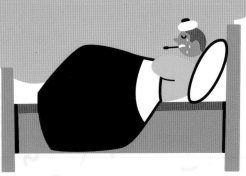

Expensive emergencies

Have you ever seen a car break down or a ceiling leak water? These kinds of things happen often. If your family has had to pay for some emergency repairs, it could mean there is less money to spend for a while.

Money addictions

An addiction to something is a very strong desire or need for it. It is defined as not having control over doing something to the point where it could be harmful to you.

Compulsive spending

Oniomania, also known as compulsive buying disorder (CBD), is a behavioral disorder that involves an uncontrollable urge to go shopping and buy things. This is increasingly taking place as online shopping.

Placing bets with friends, for example by guessing who will win a game, and purchasing mystery loot boxes in video games, are forms of gambling. They can become dangerous addictions.

Gambling

Gambling is taking part in any activity in which you risk money in the hope of winning more—but more often than not, you lose. Common forms are casinos, lotteries, scratch cards, slot machines, and betting shops.

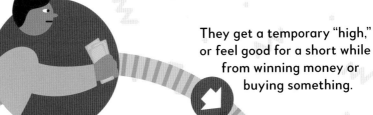

They get a temporary "high," or feel good for a short while from winning money or buying something.

People engage in gambling or compulsive spending to distract themselves from negative feelings.

Cycle of addiction

People usually take part in addictive behaviors to reduce negative feelings. It might work for a short while, but soon the negative feelings build again and so the cycle is repeated.

This leads to overspending— spending or betting more money than one can afford.

The loss of money and increasing debt leads to negative feelings of shame and guilt.

Consequences

Managing a money addiction can have many negative effects.

Constant spending leads to increasing debt that cannot be paid back.

The strain of addiction causes health problems, such as anxiety and depression.

Attempts to hide addiction results in isolation from family members and friends.

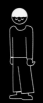

Getting help

Money addictions can be treated. People can seek advice from a doctor, or contact an organization that specializes in helping people with addictions. Self-help groups can provide support during recovery. If you think someone you know may have a money addiction, speak to an adult you can trust.

Inequality

Not everyone has the same amount of money. The difference in the amount of wealth people have is called inequality.

JUST **1%** OF PEOPLE OWN AROUND **33%** (ONE THIRD) OF ALL THE WEALTH IN THE WORLD.

The super-rich

A vast portion of the world's wealth is held by a small number of people. The wealthiest 1 per cent of people around the world are either millionaires or billionaires.

The wealth gap

The difference in wealth between richest and poorest in a particular area is often called the wealth gap. This pyramid shows how wide the wealth gap is across the whole world.

ANOTHER THIRD OF THE WEALTH BELONGS TO THE NEXT **9%** OF PEOPLE.

THE REMAINING **90%** OF THE WORLD'S POPULATION SHARE JUST A THIRD OF THE WEALTH AMONG THEM.

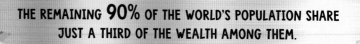

Tax dodging

Some wealthy people and companies avoid paying tax by hiding it in sneaky ways. This means a lot of money does not go back into society as it should.

You can learn more about tax on pages 66–67.

Influencing goverments

Some rich people spend money on helping their favorite politicians win elections. This may give them some power over how the government is run.

Mind the gap

So, what causes the wealth gap between the rich and poor? There are many reasons, but some are more common than others.

Poverty

Very poor people are in poverty. This means they have very little money and few possessions.

Discrimination

Discrimination is a type of inequality. It happens when someone is not given an opportunity due to their gender, race, religion, sexuality, or something else that makes them different.

Financial problems

If people lose their jobs, or are paid too little for the jobs they have, this can cause poverty.

Natural disasters

Environmental catastrophes, such as storms, floods, and droughts, can destroy homes and communities.

War and conflict

When countries are at war, many people suffer and may lose their homes and jobs.

Choosing charity

Some people choose to give money to a good cause. This is called charity.

What is a cause?

A cause is an aim or a principle. There are hundreds of causes you can help, from protecting the planet to helping people in less wealthy countries.

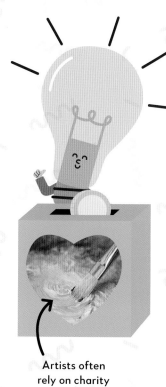

Some people think education is the most important cause.

Health charities are popular causes to donate to.

Some people choose causes that help animals and the environment.

Artists often rely on charity for funding.

Supporting a cause

There are two main ways to support a cause: donating and fundraising.

GIVING TO CHARITY IS CALLED DONATING. PEOPLE CAN DONATE MONEY, THINGS, OR THEIR TIME.

RAISING MONEY FOR CHARITY IS CALLED FUNDRAISING. THERE ARE MANY WAYS TO FUNDRAISE, SUCH AS A SPONSORED RUN.

Philanthropy

Some kind people give large amounts of money to help good causes. This is called philanthropy, and those people are known as philanthropists.

Global foundations

Some philanthropists set up organizations known as foundations. This allows them to make large, regular donations to good causes all over the world.

Li Ka-shing

Li Ka-shing is one of the most famous entrepreneurs in Asia. He has donated lots of money to try to improve healthcare.

Career: Manufacturing and real estate
Foundation: Li Ka Shing Foundation
Donated: $3.8 billion

Bill Gates

Bill Gates founded Microsoft, a huge tech company. He has used his money to fight poverty, disease, and inequality.

Career: Technology
Foundation: Bill & Melinda Gates Foundation
Donated: $5.8 billion

Oprah Winfrey

Oprah Winfrey became famous through TV, and has since donated money to causes such as improving education.

Career: Media
Foundation: Oprah Winfrey Charitable Foundation
Donated: $400 million

Your future

When people think about money, they're often thinking about the future. But exactly how much money people need for the future depends on what they want from life.

Career goals

You might want to earn lots of money in a high-paying job. Alternatively, you might be interested in a job that pays less but is more enjoyable.

Life goals

Everyone's future is different, so everyone has different money-related goals.

Be the best boss.

Have a family.

Own a yacht.

Knowing money

Throughout this book, you've seen how money can help individuals and societies. But this is just the beginning of your money journey. As you get older, you will learn more and more about money, and how it can work for you.

Retirement goals

You may want to retire as early as possible. This would mean saving a lot of money in your pension, investments, or other savings.

Travel the world.
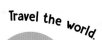

Protect the environment.

The important thing to remember is that money is a personal thing—everybody can and should spend their money in their own way.

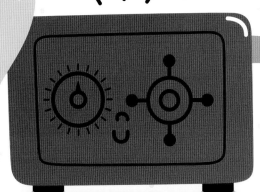

Activities

Use your money knowledge
to take on these activities.

try it yourself
TIY
try it yourself

**If you could mint your own coins or design
your own notes, what would they look like?**

Most coins are round
because it makes them
easier to handle in
machines. **What shape
would your coin be?**

Many countries
celebrate people's
achievements by
putting their faces
on banknotes.
**Who would you
celebrate on yours?**

Some banknotes are
printed with luminescent
ink that is only visible under
a UV light. This makes the notes
hard to forge. **What other security
features would you consider?**

Shin Saimdang was the first
woman to be featured on a
South Korean banknote.

**Money has changed over the years, but what
do you think it will look like in the future?**

Budget builder

Take a look at this basic budget and then try making your own.

You use this column to plan how much you **think** your expenses will cost.

Actual spending tells you how much your expenses **actually** cost.

This shows the **difference** between your budget and actual costs.

EXPENSES	BUDGETED	ACTUAL	DIFFERENCE
Food	$10	$12	- $2
Clothes	$15	$10	+ $5
Books	$5	$5	$0
Toys	$15	$10	+ $5
		Total:	+ $8

This total box shows if you have gone **over or under** your budget.

Here are some things you might want to budget for. If you have **$100** in your bank account, what things can you afford and what will you leave out of your budget?

$5

School supplies

$10

Food

$40

A new game

$15

Movie tickets

$20

New clothes

$25

A birthday present for a friend

THINK MONEY

How many of the above items are needs and how many of them are wants? Are any of them both?

Quiz

It's time to put your money knowledge to the test!

1. Which type of plant was used to make the first paper money?

a. Bamboo

b. Mulberry tree

c. Oak tree

d. Pine tree

2. What is a pension?

a. A special savings fund for retirement

b. A loan you take out for buying a house

c. A special savings fund for a new car

d. A loan you take out to go on holiday

3. If you borrow 100 coins with 10 percent interest, how many will you have to pay back?

a. 10 coins

b. 101 coins

c. 110 coins

d. 1000 coins

4. Which of the following are rules of investing?

a. Budget carefully

b. Diversify your investments

c. Be patient

d. All of the above

5. Which of these are not a good way to raise money for charity?

a. A bake sale

b. Donating clothes

c. Buying latest trends

d. A sponsored walk

Answers: 1 b; 2 a; 3 c; 4 d; 5 c

1. Inflation is always a good thing.

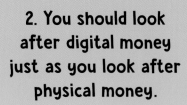

2. You should look after digital money just as you look after physical money.

3. A share is a small part of a company.

4. Everyone should spend and save their money in the same way.

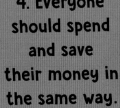

5. A bank will never ask you to transfer money to another account.

6. Investing is a quick way to make a lot of money.

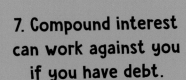

7. Compound interest can work against you if you have debt.

TRUE OR FALSE

Glossary

ATM a machine that dispenses cash and provides other banking services

balance the amount of money in a particular place, such as a savings account

bank a financial organization that is allowed to receive and loan money

bartering the exchange of goods or services without using money

borrowing receiving something with the intention of giving it back

budget a plan that helps you work out how to use money over a period of time

cash money in coins or notes

coinage metal money, or coins

cost the payment required to receive a good or service

credit the opportunity to obtain goods or services before payment, based on trust that the payment will be made in the future

currency a system of money in general use in an area or country

debt an amount of money that is owed

deflation a general reduction in the prices of things in an economy

demand people's desire to purchase a thing for a particular price

deposit a sum of money paid into a bank account

diversification a strategy that involves having a wide variety of investments

employed having a job

entrepreneur a person who sets up a business or venture

exchange rate the value of one currency compared to another

export to sell goods or services to another country

fiat money money that is backed by the government

firm a business that provides professional services

gold standard a now-abandoned system in which the value of a currency was equivalent to a set amount of gold

goods physical items that can be bought and sold

government a group of people in charge of a particular area or country

income money that is received

inflation a general increase in the prices of goods and services in an economy

interest extra money that is added to deposits or loans at a set rate

investing putting money into something with the expectation of making a profit

loan money that is borrowed

mortgage a loan used to buy property

pension a fund for people to use when they retire

philanthropy donating large amounts of money to good causes

profit money a company gains by doing business

recession a period of economic decline, when the amount of goods and services produced shrinks

redundancy losing a job because the company needs to cut costs

resources items used to make goods and offer services

salary a regular payment received by an employee in exchange for work

services jobs done in exchange for money

shares portions of ownership of a company

sponsored supporting a person by giving them money or products

supply the availability of a good or service

tax a compulsory payment to the government

trade the act of buying or selling goods or services

unemployed when someone who is capable of working is unable to find work

value how much something is worth

wealth the amount of valuable possessions or money a person has

Index

About the author: Kalpana Fitzpatrick is an award-winning journalist with extensive experience in financial journalism. She writes for newspapers, magazines and websites. Kalpana is often on TV and radio in the UK, appearing on the BBC, ITV, and Sky News.

The publisher would like to thank the following people for their help in the production of this book: Polly Goodman for proofreading; Helen Peters for the index; Ahmad Bilal, Vagisha Pushp, and Rituraj Singh for picture research; Neeraj Bhatia and Rizwan Mohd for hi-res assistance; Agey George, Katie Lawrence, Manisha Majithia, and Kathleen Teece for additional editorial; Bettina Myklebust Stovne, Victoria Palastanga, Brandie Tully-Scott, and Nehal Verma for additional design.

Picture credits